Rev Bruce Hyman

Keep blessing
Men!

THE DAY MY
DADDY DIED

Tyrone Stevenson

TABLE OF CONTENTS

FOREWORD

By John K. Jenkins Sr.

While I have six biological children, I have also been blessed to father several spiritual children in ministry, one of whom is Tyrone Stevenson. I have known Tyrone for over 20 years. As a young man, he was a dedicated member of the First Baptist Church of Glenarden, who willingly served in various ministries. He assisted me personally for a period of time and was faithful in accomplishing duties big and small. He eventually became a minister at First Baptist until answering the call to plant a church in his home community of Brooklyn, NY.

I have seen Tyrone wrestle with issues in his life and watched as he has allowed each one of them to shape and develop him into a better husband, father, son and pastor. In his book, *The Day My Daddy Died,* Tyrone deals head-on with the reality of growing up without a biological father and challenges men in his position to do the same. He argues that being "fatherless" should not be ignored, but rather addressed and used as a springboard for making sound choices that will positively impact the trajectory of the reader's life and the generations to come. Tyrone is practicing what he preaches, and his authentic transparency will captivate you throughout the book, while encouraging you to become all that you can be.

INTRODUCTION

I grew up without a father. There, I said it! The saddest part about my declaration is that many of us, especially in the African American community, have grown up without a father. We never really experienced the joy of lovingly uttering the beckoning call of "Daddy!", and receiving the self-assuring response of smiling eyes or a pair of warm outstretched arms. Boys of this fatherless tribe, find ourselves as grown men living in a life shaped by a dangerous lie. What lie could that be, you ask? The one that erupts from our mouths when someone or something touches our fatherless wound. In an attempt to mask our pain, we blurt out, "I don't need a father" or "I don't need a man to teach me how to be a man."

Deep down inside, every one of us knows that is not true. I firmly believe that "no man becomes a man without another man." Moreover, the man that you choose to emulate is the man that you will become. A father is a necessary part of a boy's development because he is the external picture of where that boy comes from. He is an anchor to that little boy's definition of manhood. Therefore, the absence of a father creates a tremendous wound in the life of a fatherless boy and when this wound is left untreated, it creates pain that is passed on from generation to generation. Fathers are necessary, period! Despite what culture tries to portray, each one of us—at every stage of our life from childhood on through—reaches for our daddy.

This book was written to encourage you, the now grown-up 'men of the fatherless tribe'. It is my hope that no matter where you are in your journey, that you realize that despite all of your accomplishments that there is nothing more important or powerful than being a living daddy to your children. I want this book to begin a real dialogue between men of all ages about our pain and how to deal with it. The goal is not to repeat the issues and shortcomings of our past. My prayer is that we become healed, whole, and healthy men who stop bleeding on the next generation and start leading the next generation.

I invite you to go on this journey with me, and together, we are going to come out stronger than ever. We will be empowered with the goal to make those who we care about, the best versions of themselves. There is an old African proverb that says "If you close your eyes to facts, you will learn through accidents." It is time to break the closed-eye culture of denial that breeds accidents and give life to a new one that creates mighty men of valor, fuelled by truths.

CHAPTER 1: YOUR CHOICE

HOW WILL YOU BE REMEMBERED?

What will be your legacy? Will it be your job? The same one that will fill your position a week after you die? Maybe it will be your money, cars, jewelry, or houses. Please don't get me wrong, those things have their place. However, I would suggest that they should not be in first place. Okay, how about this question. What do you truly value? Are the things that you listed, different from the ones before? I believe that your happiness resides in your answers to those two questions. When you really examine your answers, you will discover what you truly want to be remembered for when you die.

I found myself trying to answer these questions after I watched a friend go through a very messy divorce. He spent many years of his marriage messing up. Then when he finally realized the importance of his marriage and decided to turn his life around, it was too late. Right when he was willing to fight for his marriage, his wife had arrived at the point where she no longer wanted to be married to him. Sadly, the story doesn't end there. The court proceeding began but my friend decided to close his eyes to the reality of the divorce. Acting out of a reality that he created for himself, he refused to hire a lawyer and then exclaimed: "I don't need a lawyer because I don't want a divorce."

Well, I watched as the walls of my friend's reality collapsed around him. This front seat view into the most painful period of my friend's life served as a nice attention-grabbing slap. Now wide awake, I recognized that I didn't want that for my life nor for my family. I decided at that moment that I wanted my legacy to positively impact the people who will feel my absence in their lives until their death. To make this a reality I had to go on a journey to change the narratives that defined my life at that time. I wish I could say that my friend's divorce was my only wake-up call. Honestly, my journey has been riddled with several other wake-up calls. All of which have helped me to create a healthier definition of my life and my legacy. Please allow me to share a few with you.

Adjusting My Lens

Once I decided to make a change, I reluctantly accepted that I would have to look back before I would be able to move forward. I had to look back and engage the elephant in my life. I had to acknowledge the pain I was in. I did this by embracing the gift of self-awareness. I needed to come to grips with this truth, that the common denominator in the things that were going on in my life was me. I made the decision to stop pretending that I was immune to pain. I had spent too many years lying to myself. It was time to put to sleep a major source of my pain, the lie that was cleverly disguised, as "I do not need a male role model in my life." It was time to stop crippling myself by believing that I would be unable to admit that I wanted my father without discounting my single mother's love for me. I know that I am not the only man that carried this weight out of his childhood, through his youth, and into his manhood. Too many men are inflicting pain on themselves and others because we are afraid of becoming another source of pain for the women who sacrificed so much for us. We quietly convince ourselves that if we acknowledge our need for our absentee fathers then we are belittling our mothers who were present. Well, one of my first steps forward was to literally tell myself that this was the furthest thing from the truth.

After I put that untruth to rest, my next step was to acknowledge my gratitude for the women who raised me. However, unlike before, my appreciation was still allowed to live alongside my ability to embrace my need for my father. One of the most damaging statements I remember dealing with in silence was on Mother's Day hearing women say "I have been both mother and father." Pause. My dear and loving sisters, let me talk with you for a second. Please, please, please, as you read this book decide to stop pushing this false narrative. This statement does not have any basis in reality. It is one drenched in hurt that damages the already fragile psyche of the emotionally depleted and already deeply pained man. Moreover, that statement suggests the idea of interchangeable parental roles in which a mother can be a father and a father can be a mother. I am not an advocate of that idea.

I am a firm supporter of the beauty and importance of the diversity of the parental roles. Let me explain it this way. If my house was on fire, I would not call the police, although I could. I would call the fire department. You could argue that both groups are rescuers who have been trained to preserve life. While your argument would be valid, I would argue that while they may share a life-preserving purpose, they use different tools in response to different threats to achieve the same goal. Similarly, while a mother and father have the same responsibility of developing their children into well-rounded productive and loving human beings, they are equipped with distinct, yet complementary tools to respond to their children's needs. So yes, both a mother and a father are needed to parent a child. There are times when the tools of one might be needed more than that of the other.

Okay, so now that I had put on my big boy pants and dealt with the source of my pain. I was finished, right? Not really. Although I had acknowledged its existence and I identified what was feeding it, I was now tasked with the challenge of combing through my life to see where I may have allowed it to take up residence. How many years had I been living with pain as a functional handicap? Most of my life. So, then it is only logical that it would take more than seeing the lie for what it was. I would also have to do the work of evicting the behaviors and the thoughts that informed those behaviors. If not, then all I did was to shine the spotlight on the intruder and then turn my back. Now in eviction mode, I had to ask myself if I wanted my pain and its symptoms to be my legacy. That question started me down a daunting path and smack into another question. How did I want to be remembered when I died? Yes, scary question. News flash! We are all going to die. Forgive my being crass.

Wait. Nope, I meant it.

I said that because we often forget how short life really is. I say "we" because I have lived most of my life under the false narrative that I was only as good as what I accomplished. I had never really slowed down to take the time to fully understand what makes me happy, outside of hollow accomplishments. Like the rest of the world, I was caught up in the rat race. A race with the sole purpose of collecting more stuff to leave to my family who would remember me because of all the stuff I left them. Now doesn't that sound crazy? Yet it is exactly what most of us are doing. We are working ourselves into early graves and giving our family the things that don't matter while denying them the one thing that matters most—us. This brought me to a 'eureka moment', that had me embracing the reality that life is short and that I did not have to accept living a life crippled by a passing wound. It was actually the key to finding my happiness now, while I was still kicking. This ultimately freed me to tell myself that I had every right to redefine what happiness meant for me, void of the lies of my yesterdays. So, it is my hope that you would join me in embracing this truth. Nobody can make us happy. Rather our happiness is a gift that we must find and define for ourselves. Happiness in our self will always escape us until we identify the things that we truly value, and once identified we must be willing to fight for those values. When we know what makes us happy, we truly know what we value, and then life decisions are easier to make. I say to my children, "when you know what is important to you then decisions are easy".

Choosing How I Am Remembered

I went through a season in my life when I challenged myself to identify the core values that defined me. As I became clearer about my core values and began to apply them in my day-to-day life a curious thing started to happen. I realized that I was a much happier person. Amazingly, it was then and only then that I was able to comfortably answer how I wanted to be remembered when I died. It was another eureka moment. I had begun to live a value filled life and that made me happy. There it was! When I died, I wanted to be remembered for how I lived not what I left behind.

My happiness is governed by three core values.

1. I want to be remembered as a spiritually grounded and emotionally healthy man. My spiritual grounding and growth are the center of who I am as a person. My decisions, direction, and determinations are all centered on my loving personal relationship with God. There is nothing more important to me than my spiritual and emotional health. I have learned that when I am not spiritually and emotionally grounded nothing else really matters. I am happiest and my family is most fulfilled when I am healthy in these two areas. There is something to be said about embarking on a journey toward being a healthy and well-rounded person. It requires work and dedication but it is worth it. My prayer time is the most beneficial thing that I engage in on a daily basis. Despite the stigma in the African

American community towards mental health, emotional wholeness can be achieved through the use of counselling services. I am a firm advocate of counselling as a resource in finding happiness. I spend time with a therapist and the benefits have been amazing for my family and for my personal growth.

2. I want to be remembered as a parental coach for my children. I had the awesome opportunity to meet Magic Johnson at an Urban League event. I asked him if he would rather be remembered as a superhero or a coach. He said a coach without hesitation. From that moment I began to model the skills of a coach. That day I recognized that my ability to positively impact my children and their future was dependent on my ability to

balance the role of parent and coach. So, when my daughter began to attend university, I sat them down and explained to them that my role as their parent would start to look and feel more like a coach. I explained that as their parent my role was to give and enforce boundaries so that they could learn and grow. Now that they were sufficiently grown my role had transitioned into that of a coach who would show them what to do and be their sounding board as they made decisions. Having this talk with my daughters was extremely important because as a child I was not afforded the opportunity to make any decisions whatsoever. Therefore, I made many mistakes, mistakes that I do not want my children to make.

3. I want to be remembered as a husband

who was available to his wife. This value is tied to the first one. For many years I was unavailable to my wife because I was so emotionally broken and depleted. I was unable to love myself, let alone love her. Instead, I took the love and turned it towards the stuff I collected. This value keeps me from ever putting things and people before the most important relationship I will have with another human being. Remaining available to my wife allows me to learn her nuances and fall in love with her over and over again. An invaluable gift. This value might well be the most important of the three because as a parent-coach I am preparing my children to leave the nest one day. That would mean that at some point it will just be my wife and I. Therefore, she deserves 100% availability. Brothers, the women in your life need you to be vulnerable and we need to be able to give them that. I work to be vulnerable with my wife in every way possible, especially emotionally. It requires work, but nothing worth having comes easy.

So, what is it that you want to be remembered for? What is the legacy you want to leave on the earth? No matter how old or young you are you still have time to change the narrative. I encourage you to take on the challenge of identifying your core values. Once you have done that, go a step further and connect them with how you would like to be remembered. When I went on this journey it was scary because I had to look deeply at my true self as opposed to the person I wanted to believe I was. In order to successfully complete this challenge, I had to ask my family how they saw me. You guessed it, the answers were not always pleasant. Yet, despite the hard work of putting to sleep some distorted self-perceptions, I kept at it. I continued on because I realized that it is the work I needed to do in order to change the narrative of my current life. I am glad that I stuck with it because my today is much brighter than my yesterday.

My Life, The Unimaginable Dream

Today at the age of 48, I am the father of three. My oldest princess, as of the writing of this book, just graduated from university. My middle princess is in the midst of her college experience and our surprise prince is 10. I have only been married once to my Queen, Terrie, who has been with me for 25 years, despite all of my flaws. She has supported me and has been helping me to grow into the man I am becoming. I am currently the founding pastor of our church in Brooklyn that began with only nine people. That number included my family of four at the time. All I had was a few people and a vision of something better for the community. Today with plans for expansion, there are 600 members who regularly attend one of our two locations.

I have had many successes in life that span my time in the military and in the legal and banking sector. I was even academically blessed when I was given the opportunity to complete my master's degree, without a bachelor's degree. Of course, I had to prove my ability to successfully navigate graduate work. Well, prove I did when I graduated with a 3.8 GPA. This was major for someone from a family where college degrees are rare. God has given me the ability to be a good manager of money and that created financial security for my family. I am immensely grateful to be able to provide for my family. I think my wife would agree that today I am a good husband and a good father to our children.

However, my rosy today had a thorny beginning. Things were very different back then. Most of my early life was overshadowed by the haunting thought that I would not live to see my 25th birthday. Looking back on my childhood, my younger self would not have been able to imagine my world today. Yet, I recognize that ultimately the blessings of my today are direct results of my decision to 1) acknowledge my pain and 2) to take action steps, although difficult, to ensure that my pain did not become the legacy I passed on to my children.

CHAPTER 2: THE WOUND

THE DAY EVERYTHING CHANGED

I did not play sports as a boy. If I was not in church, I basically was home. As a child, my home life revolved around what was happening at the church. I remember that day so clearly. All the children on our block went roller-skating, including my seven sisters. I wanted to go with the other kids, but my mother did not want me to go.

At first, I thought maybe my mom wanted to spend time with me. I guess that was half right, one of my parents did want to spend time with me but it was not my mom. It was my father. After being left behind, my mother explained to me that my father was coming to the house. That was all I needed to hear. I got super excited!

My father wanted to come and spend time with me. Finally, this man who I needed so desperately in my life, wanted to be with me! I remember feeling so excited while I was sitting on the porch waiting for him. I think that was the only time in my life that I ever felt like I did not have to do anything for him to spend time with me. Unlike other times, I was not in trouble and he was not coming to see my mom. He wanted to be with me! Then my imagination took over, and a daydreaming I went. Would he take me to the movies? Oh, no! Coney Island? Maybe we would just ride around in his car and people would see me with my Father! Yes!!!

Hours passed and there I was, sitting on the

porch but he never came. Then the inner battle started. I fought back the emotions inside me and tried not to think about the last time he did not show up. No, I don't want to think about that time because that time he never showed and I was sexually molested. Nope, I don't want to think about that. Yet, time kept ticking and my father was nowhere in sight. As my excitement died, my thoughts began to shift and I started to pray, "Please, God. Don't let this be happening again." Then my frustration started to build up, and I decided that I had enough. I got up off the porch and went inside where my mom was entertaining some guests. Blinded by my frustration I said to my mom, "I want to go do something," and she said, "You can't, your father is coming." Now let me clarify something, I was not the child who normally spoke back to my mother and my mother was definitely not the woman that you raised your voice too. Yet, my response to her was, "It has been hours!"

Then suddenly, like a pressure cooker going off, all of my frustration exploded out of me. I remember saying something to the effect of, "What makes you think he's coming? He never comes. He always says he's coming but he never comes!" For a moment there, the boy that never answered his mother back forgot that he was in a house filled with adults. I looked at everyone and they were all silent. I looked back at my mom and I knew that she was getting ready to whoop me. I was going to get the beating of my life, but I didn't care! Moreover, I was not finished giving my mother a piece of my mind. So I continued and said to her, "I don't care. He's dead to me!" I ran into the bathroom and locked the door and broke down. I was in major meltdown mode. I was kicking the walls and yelling at the top of my lungs. I was hurting and I did not care if the entire world outside of the bathroom heard my anguish. It was at that moment that my head started to ache. It felt as if it was going to explode. Now I can hear people outside the door. They are trying to get into the bathroom but I was not finished screaming and crying.

Wait. No, I was finished, I wanted it to end, period. I started going through the medicine cabinet looking for something that would end it all. All the pain, all the agony. I wanted it, no I needed it to stop. So, I continued my quest. Maybe, there was there something sharp? No, wait, maybe there was some pills that I could take that would allow me to end my life? There had to be something. There!

My eyes locked on a bottle of aspirin and I reached for it. My intent to end my life at that moment was so strong that swallowing the pills would be too slow. So I decided to crush them up and snort it so that it would enter my system faster. Nothing was getting in between me and my goal to end this pain. A pain so overwhelming that only my death would stop the hurting.

Then after a while, I remember calmness seeping in and covering me. I slowly got up off the floor and I looked in the mirror. Looking back at me was a tear-drenched face with a pair of bloodshot eyes. I splashed my face with water and looked at myself again in the mirror. Then I pointed at the face looking back at me and said, "Today is the last day you will want anybody who doesn't want you," and with that, I opened the door. I walked out like nothing ever happened but something did happen at that moment. Something in me had changed. The Tyrone that walked out of that bathroom no longer wanted anyone who didn't want him. He had made up his mind.

That was the day my father died.

At least to me, he was dead. Mentally I went through the grief of my father's death. I closed the casket of my memory of that day and buried it deep inside of me. From time to time I would revisit the gravesite of that day but my father was dead and I buried him. Interestingly, I never got rid of the shovel though. So, from that day on I walked through life armed with my shovel ready to bury the things that required me to become that vulnerable little boy again. That day I joined the fatherless tribe and my life was never the same again.

Never Enough

While I never knew who I was, I knew that I was full of internal anger. I was quiet, but I was a powder keg ready to explode. I was extremely unhappy. If you asked most of the people who knew me when I was growing up, they would have a hard time believing that statement. That was because even as a child, I had mastered the art of covering up my feelings. I am the seventh of eight children and the only male, yes seven girls and one boy. Yet, I grew up very lonely, very quiet, and with no voice. At an early age, I learned that my voice never really mattered. I was not good at relationships and I did not have many friends. The loneliness I felt was deep, and although I was able to hide it behind a fake confidence, inside...I was broken. As the only boy in the house, I had my own room and my own toys. I was surrounded by people but still lonely. I hated my life and I hated myself. In fact, if you were to ask me now for one good childhood memory, I would not be able to think of one. My childhood was not much of a "childhood" from as far back as I can remember.

At a very young age, I had already learned that work was important. So I did my job well. As a child, my job was to be a good student. So I was an excellent student because I believed that if I did a good job, I would get love in return. I was only lovable when I handled my business. That was how I understood love. Love was the result of my achievements. This belief was reinforced by early interactions with my dad. Interactions that only occurred when I was not doing well in school, when I was not being lovable. Feeling unloved was not reserved for my relationship with my dad. I did not feel loved in any other area in my life. My friendships were based on things that I could do for my friends. At church, I felt that the people who loved me loved me because I was good at studying the Bible. The reward for my achievement was to encourage me to start preaching at the age of 12. A reward that turned up the pressure and intensified my feelings of loneliness. Sadly, in their attempts to love me the people in my life unknowingly kept feeding a very unhealthy definition of love. One that equated to my ability to give or excel. The pressure to give and excel was shouldered along with the burden of being the man of the house.

CHAPTER 3: THE RESPONSE

TRYING TO MEASURE UP

My mother and father were never married. Therefore, out of my eight siblings, I share the same biological parents with only one other sibling, my younger sister. Growing up, I never witnessed what it meant to be a man. I did not know what a father did. I tried to guess what that would look like as I tried to be the man of the house. However, all that was, was me putting an incredible amount of pressure on myself. It was the perfect recipe for failure.

Unknowingly, single moms make the mistake of telling their young boys that they are the men of the house. This statement asks a young boy to assume the responsibility of man, a task that he is not equipped to carry. Especially, if he has never seen his father model how to carry that responsibility. If I had to define my life growing up, the word pressure would be the word I would use. I was not old enough to be a man but yet I had too much pressure on me to be a boy.

Whenever I would hear my mother talking about her worries over paying the rent, I would feel the pressure of trying to find a way to pay it—even without a job. I was constantly fighting an inner struggle, as I tried to figure out how I would fulfill my 'man of the house' duties. As if that was not enough, I also had to deal with the boy who would watch his friends interact with their fathers and then wonder if he had to be both "man of the house" and "the father of the house." As the only male in our house, did it fall on me? Then with all of these unanswered questions, I had to deal with the reality that I was a child. How could I do those things in a child's body? Feeling the pressure of having an adult male's responsibility while never having any clear images of what it meant to be a man, was so hard to deal with. There was just this constant pressure with no answer and no relief. This unrelenting pressure was coupled with a mother who unintentionally but continuously, knocked me down. My mother is a strong woman. Her life demanded that of her but often times, her strength left me feeling emasculated. It could be that there were moments when my mother needed me to respond in a way that was more fitting for my father, but he was not there. This pressure did not make me a diamond, It was creating a young boy that was about to snap.

Terrible Isolation

For much of my life, I didn't know how to build deep relationships. In fact, I had become the master of camouflaging my feelings and I did want to learn how to connect. I would have people thinking I was their best friend, but if they spoke or acted in a way that I did not like, it was over. Just like that, they were cut off and dead to me. I would pull out my shovel and bury it, done! I remember one time, I even ended an engagement without letting the girl know that I was done. I was the emotionally walking dead. There was a deadness inside of me that prevented me from building deep relationships with anybody. I was just waiting for them to be the next person that I used my shovel on.

Then my amazing wife walked into my life. When we first met, we talked on the phone for nine weeks before we ever laid eyes on one another. We mailed our photos to one another and timed it so that they would arrive on the day we planned to meet. Well, you should have guessed it. Mr. Shovel King had other ideas. Like an addict, I was itching for a reason to stop talking to her. Well, that is when the script flipped and then something different in my life happened. Something I had never allowed myself to experience before. We decided on a date and time to meet. As the date approached, I was ready with my shovel. The plan was that I would drive up to her college, Georgia Southern University, and meet her at 10:00 am. When the date finally arrived, I did not show up. I went and did something else that day. It was not until 11:00 pm that night that I decided to call. I flippantly told her something came up and that I would try to come see her again tomorrow. The next thing I heard was "You don't know me, but you can't treat me with such disrespect. You are somebody I don't want to meet. Don't come here." Then the phone clicked. Dial tone!

Wait! This was different… Someone finally wanted to be with me and there I was with my stupid shovel trying to kill the situation by rejecting her first. Why? Because I was too scared that she would reject me. This was new territory for me and I was amazed! There I was looking at the phone and asking myself, "Did she really just hang up on me?" The phone clicking in my ears, jolted me into action. I was so shocked that I immediately called her back and said "Wait! Don't hang up, I just want to come and see you." Nope, she was not entertaining my shenanigans and she made it quite clear. She said "I don't care what you do" and hung up again! That was it. She had my attention.

Now I am talking to myself, "Okay she does not know how I look. She does not know if I have money. She just wants to meet me." This was one of the few times in my life where I felt this person was interested in me and not what I could offer them. The next thing I knew, I was in my car. I drove from Homerville, Georgia to Statesboro, Georgia at midnight! This was on the back roads with no lights and in those days those roads were not friendly to a young brash black man in a speeding sports car. It did not matter, I was on a mission! When I made it to her dorm, she barely wanted to open the door. Finally, when she did, I took her to breakfast and we sat up all night and talked and watched the sunrise. It was one of the happiest times of my life, and 28 years later she is still the love of my life. I found a person that I could establish a different relationship with. From that point on, I was different, but only with my wife and then our children.

I had set myself a goal for how I wanted my marriage to be. I was only going to be married once and then if I was going to have children, I was going to be married to the mother. It was going to be different for my wife and my children. I had different rules for them. I lived so much of my life with a dichotomy of living one way with them and another way with the rest of the world, but I couldn't build a deeper relationship even with my wife and children and I began to realize I had to get better at it. That was when I found the desire to want to change.

The Poison Called Bitterness

Too often we live our lives based on the bitterness of our past. If we are not careful, we will run the risk of being defined by that same bitterness. It will hold us back. We have to understand that we have to move beyond the bitterness. No man is going to become a man without a man. It just does not happen that way. Men, we have to identify our bitterness and its source and consequences and then decide to engage a new standard of living. If not, we will stay stuck in the bitterness of our past and what's worse, is that the people who have nothing to do with our bitterness, our children, and spouses will pay the greatest price. It was my bitterness that made me a walking emotional zombie before I met my wife. Unfortunately, my wife was not the medicine to all of my bitterness because I still had a lot of self-work to do. Before I started to do that personal work, I reserved the consequences of my bitterness for everyone except for my wife and kids, or so I thought.

When I need to remind myself of what is at stake, I paint the following picture: "Bitterness is like me drinking bleach and hoping that the other person dies." Although, I told myself that I buried my emotions when I buried my father that day, like my friend and his divorce, I was closing my eyes to reality. The hurt of my past had grown into a bitterness that prevented me from building healthy relationships. With my eyes closed to this reality, I was using my bitterness to destroy myself, hoping that father that I buried would get the message. This toxic response to my past wound was preventing me from being all that I could be for my wife and children. I was sacrificing the source of my current happiness to prove to my father, something that I did not even really know I was trying to prove. So here I was a married man erroneously living my life based on the lie that I had made it this far without a man guiding me in my life. When in actuality, the bitterness that I carried around from my father's absence was causing me to rob myself and others of the love that I should have been able to give and receive. I had begun to realize that moment in the bathroom many years ago was not dead. Rather, it was haunting my life now as a bitter shadow. No matter how many mental funerals I had for my father, I was still that disappointed little boy who wanted to barter his father's love as his achievements. It was then that I told myself, "He is you and you're him. As much as you don't like it and fight against it, you're becoming the thing you despise."

Yes, I did not father a bunch of babies, but I was still emotionally unavailable to the people who meant the most to me. I had reasoned that because I had grown up so poor, that loving the people in my life only required me to provide them with money, houses, and other material things. I was living as an adult on the outside, but on the inside, I was like a seven-year-old child who now had money. Every time my wife and I would get into an argument, I would run down the list of things that I bought for them like the house, the cars, and the private school for the kids. That list of accomplishments was like a board that I could hold up to show that I was being a man, but what I was really doing was making huge mistakes. I was leading my life down a road that was going to end up one day with one of my children in the bathroom kicking the walls and crying because they hated me. I was giving them material things that my father never gave me but I was not giving them the things that my children really needed. Yet again I found myself at the point where I realized that I had to make a shift in life. I had to find a way to change because it was not enough to just make a bunch of money and give the people in my life a bunch of things. My family and my future deserved more, they deserved more of me!

CHAPTER 4: THE RECOVERY

A PARADIGM SHIFT

Scene:

I was drunk, high and I was seeing red. Then my favorite song, Straight Outta Compton, comes on and my ears zero in on the verse "AK 47 is my tool. Don't make me act a fool." That was my trigger button! I went into my apartment, got my gun and clip, loaded it, and came back outside. Everybody was drinking, smoking, and enjoying themselves. I made the gun ready and stood behind my friend as he was dancing, alcohol in the hand, and then everyone got quiet. I knew at that moment that I was going to kill him. I don't remember his exact words but I remember another friend saying, "She's not worth it." Letting that go in one ear and go out the other, I took the clip out and ejected the round from the chamber. Then I said to him, "Do we understand each other?" I was so close to ending two lives—his and mine. Everything in me wanted to pull that trigger because he had embarrassed me.

That was when I told myself, "Tyrone you don't kill someone because they embarrass you." At the time I was living in Florida, an open carry state, and I was in the military. I owned a lot of guns, living what I called the "thug life". Earlier that day I had found out that one of my friends had been messing with my girlfriend at the time. So, I decided to deal with him at one of our impromptu outside parties. All I can remember is feeling so angry. I was going to kill him because violence and anger was my way of dealing with the hurt that I felt in that situation. I had grown up and replaced the crushed aspirins with a gun and this time I set on taking someone else with me. Moreover, I was taking a definite step towards becoming the very thing that I had hated. It shook me and I knew at that moment that I had to start making some changes.

I had to go through many scenes like the one above before I seriously made the decision to be a better person. A couple years after that scene I found myself on the tails of being charged for a murder that I did not commit. That experience opened my eyes a little bit more, but not enough for me to be willing to face the pain of getting better. Then I got into a car accident while driving an uninsured vehicle, while I was stationed at the prestigious Pentagon. I was working on the "E" ring (known as the ring of power) and here came a police officer that escorted me out of the office to be arrested. As if that was not enough, I was informed that I was being charged for the accident and being sued. Here I am, a newly married man, who just purchased his first house, and I was being sued for around $100,000. Without delay, I hired a lawyer and I remembered him telling me, "You have a house so they know there is something to get." But for me, the only thing that mattered was my family. That experience was the last straw. It really humbled me and forced me to admit to myself that I was not the man I thought I was. It took a while to stick but I finally accepted that I had to learn what it meant to be a healthy well-balanced man.

I had to begin the journey of moving from just having things to really truly having relationships. I created for myself a mantra to move from the bitterness into true happiness: *bitter people don't get better and better people refuse to get bitter*! I still use that mantra to inform my life today. Bitterness was my fuel and it was stopping me from getting better. Now that I had that golden nugget of truth, I replayed it over and over in my head. *Bitter people don't get better and better people refuse to get bitter*! Better people refuse to get bitter. It became the soundtrack to my journey down a new road. It allowed me to come to grips with how bitter I had been and it encouraged me to find a way to become a better person. I was able to start freeing myself from my attachment to things. I was able to declare that "I am more than a house and I am more than the things that I can provide." This freedom from my material attachments helped me to confidently state that "If we lost the lawsuit and we lost everything. We can always get another house. We can get another car." The most important realization during this process was the fact that my family would still love me without those things. However, that did not dismiss the fact that I still needed to learn to deal with the pain in my life before that pain solidified as my plan.

Where I was emotionally in life when those three scenarios played out, makes me think of the story of David in the Bible. David has always been the person in the Bible that I identify with the most. David was on the rooftop of his house when he should have been at war. Instead of doing his duty as King his decision to not deal with the pain of the death of his son had him doing things that he knew he should not have done. He was running from his pain but face smack into trouble. Despite my outer appearance, I was still that hurt and disappointed 13-year-old kicking the wall. What I needed to do was take away the remote control from the boy and give it to the man. To do that I had to first recognize the bitterness that was causing me to misuse the real gifts that I had been given in life. I was not using those gifts to get better, instead, I was just getting increasingly bitter.

Finding Authentic Examples

Often as men, we model our lives after an impression we get from somebody. For most of my adult life, I was basing my life on my impression of a dead man. I would succeed at one thing or another and then leave it. I succeeded in the military and then I left. I succeeded in the banking sector and then I left that too. I had to find something that was part of a future that I could not leave, and for me, that was my wife and my children. But, I was still trying to find the man that I was supposed to be. I did not know who I was at 22. I was married to an amazing woman but I still felt like a seven-year-old inside.

One day I was talking to a friend, who happens to be a therapist, about the torture I was feeling internally. He opened my eyes with this statement, "The legitimate unmet needs of the child become the agenda of the adult," and those words were the frame of the life I was living. My needs as a child were dictating my future as an adult. I was living out the very steps I resented, looking in the mirror and seeing it staring at me—the man I had buried. Here I was sabotaging my future because of the absence of a father I thought I did not need, but who deep down I was still looking for. I was becoming exactly like him and I had to find a way for things to be different. Up to this point in my life, I had always underestimated the power and importance of strong male role models. I decided to end that. I went out on a limb and over the course of years, I began to learn how to be vulnerable with other men. I began to seek out men with their own issues, but healthier than I was. I understood that I could learn from them as I tried to heal the child that I had left on the bathroom floor all those years ago. I am well aware that there is no such thing as a perfect man. Nevertheless, I needed to get around men who would walk with me and helped me to identify the missing pieces so that I could put this puzzle together. I did not need a training program—

that came later, I just needed what most men lack, strong healthy male friendships.

Hearing men say, "No, that's not what you do. This is how, as a man, you deal with that…" was an eye-opening experience for me. I remember going to a baseball game for the first time. I was in my late twenties or early thirties. I went with one of my good friends, Vince, and his father. We were watching a no-hitter but because this was my first baseball game, I had no concept of what was going on. I was sitting there thinking to myself, "What the hell, dude? Why are you even here? How is this fun?" The game was not exciting to me so I began to watch Vince and his father interact. They were talking with each other about the no-hitter. I did not understand why they were excited. But as I watched, what I observed was pure male intentional conversation for the purpose of bonding. Then it hit me. A big part of becoming a man was having healthy male relationships, not big performances. Wait, so forming healthy male relationship would just require me to engage in simply a dialogue with another male? I could do that, right? The excitement of seeing a no-hitter and wondering if anybody's going to be able to hit the ball in that game. The simplicity of that was absolutely foreign to me. Until that moment, I really had no frame of reference for a man who could be around men and not have to perform. He would be free to just be. I liked that. If there was one thing I could appreciate, it was doing away with pressure. I had sufficient pressure growing up. So, I came to realize that becoming a man is authentically recognizing that we are more than what we have and more than what we do.

Learning To F.L.Y.

The valued-filled life that I live today would not have been possible without one of the greatest lessons I have ever learned. I said earlier in the book that "a man does not become a man without another man" and I really believe that. God really blessed me with great men to help me make the changes in my life that have put me on the road to wholeness. There is one man that I must mention at this point because without him I am certain that I would not be writing this book, married, pastoring, or walking this journey. That man is John K. Jenkins, the Senior Pastor of First Baptist Church of Glenarden in Maryland. He has served as my spiritual father for more than 20 years and the wisdom and grace God has given him for me leaves me speechless, grateful, and humbled.

Over fifteen years ago, he decided that he wanted to be a pilot. When he got his license I was one of the first people that he took flying. Up until this point, I had kept him well informed about my daddy issue. He taught me the lesson that pulled it all together for me.

One day while flying in his plane I was lamenting the turmoil of my fatherlessness and about my inability to deal with the resulting pain. I explained that I was at the end of my rope and I did not know what to do. Then he asked me a profound question. He said, "Do you know what makes this plane fly?" I thought for a moment and then talked about the engine and aerodynamics. He chuckled and said "No. What makes the plane fly are a set of principles and here they are. If the lift is greater than the weight, and the thrust is greater than the drag, the plane will fly." He continued to talk but even after I left his presence I could not shake the illustration of what makes a plane fly. And then it hit me, another eureka moment. So long as what is taking me up is stronger than what is pulling me down and what is pushing me forward is stronger than what is pulling me back, I too would fly. Then I applied that truth to the changes I needed to make in my life. I would suggest that you ask yourself what is weighing you down and pushing you back. Once you answer that question truthfully, you need to find what lifts you and what pushes you. Lastly, make sure the lift and the push are stronger than the weight and the drag. Then, my brother, you are cleared to fly! Those were the steps that taught me how to F.L.Y. Those questions helped me to decide to Forgive, Love, and Yield because those three things are stronger than anything I can face.

Forgive. The hardest lesson for me to learn was forgiveness. This required me to forgive with the understanding that there are people who have let me down in the past and that there will be people who will let me down in the future, but no matter what happens, I still need to forgive them. I need to release them. Refusing to forgive is like drinking bleach. We need to stop drinking that bleach and hoping that it is going to somehow affect another person. Instead, we should start living to heal the hurt. We have to stop using the fact that it was 'not our fault' as an excuse to remain broken. I realized that un-forgiveness was weighing me down and keeping me from going forward. I embraced that forgiving my father was not letting him off the hook, but rather it was letting me off the hook. Forgiveness allowed me to leave room for the next step, which was love.

Love. I also realized that I needed to love to point that it might hurt. I needed to be ready to release my father from the prison I was holding him in. I want you to recognize that love is a choice! I had to find something that I could say to myself whenever I came face to face with the pain of my predicament. I would say, "I do not blame my father, he did the best he could with what he knew." Those words helped me to both release and love my father at the same time.

Yield. Lastly, I needed to learn the lesson of how and when to yield. To yield is to relinquish or give up something, it is to give way to arguments, demands, or pressures. I needed to yield my right to be eternally angry with my dad. I needed to give up my right to be right. Too often we hold on to being right as a badge of honor, thereby becoming the victimizer. With this badge, we beat the offending person over the head with the fact that we are right. I had to learn to be alright with the fact that I was right while at the same time not needing the validation of making sure everyone knew I was right. You must yield what you see as your right to be angry, bitter, and hurt by letting it go. I say it this way "it is what it is, but it doesn't have to stay like it is!" Learning to F.L.Y was the liberation I needed to soar above my pain, anger, hurt, and emotional distress so that I could live not what I saw but what I did not see, but always wanted.

Today my father is 88 years old. I have had

the opportunity to spend time with him. We are not as close as I wish we could be. I cannot tell you that we have a great relationship now because we don't. In spite of that, I was able to heal many hurts with my father. I was able to take him to the Hilton Head hotel where he had worked for many years as a groundskeeper. I reserved the largest room in the hotel just for him. I picked him up and I let him have anything he wanted that entire weekend. I remember when we were checking in at the front desk, the man said, "We have the presidential suite reserved for you." My father was so surprised. He said, "When I worked here, we were not even allowed on that floor." I said to my father, "Well, not only are you allowed on that floor, but you are also going to be staying there." You see, as I learned to get better, rather than be bitter, I was able to make that change. I remember on that trip after I had shared some of the feelings I had about him while I was growing up, he asked me, "If you felt that way about me, why would you do all of this?" And I simply said to him, "You don't get better by being bitter." Bitter people don't get better and better people refuse to get bitter. We may never have the father-son relationship I dreamed of growing up, but I can genuinely say that I love my father.

Recently, I was blessed to purchase a Tesla. I drove it over to visit my dad. He has now lost his eyesight and his health is failing. I was so excited to describe to him what it was like to drive what may be one of the most exciting cars, definitely the best electric car on the market today. It was refreshing, we just talked like men. I rubbed his head and told him, "I love you, old man!" He responded, "I'm not the old man, you are" and we laughed like men.

This book is my way of saying to my father, that I do love him and that I have already forgiven him. I am now able to help people in a place that I never saw growing up. I can create a reality that is different from the reality that I was born into. I hope you believe that you really can be what you did not see. I actually thank my father for the gift of being able to move beyond the bitterness that was my life, and for being able to say I have no bitterness in my heart towards him. I am no longer drinking bleach, hoping that he will die. I am a good man today and I will continue to strive to be better. My life is no longer defined by the day my daddy died.

Made in the USA
Middletown, DE
03 February 2019